An Emotional Rollercoaster

An Autobiography

By Dale Preston

Preface

I encourage you to read my story with an open mind that anything is possible. To be honest, I never thought about sharing my life story because I'm nobody special, famous or overly successful. But, after numerous recommendations and encouragement from friends, I finally found the courage and fortitude to do so.

I will refrain from mentioning any specific names of people and places in order to respect their anonymity and my privacy. At times, however I may use pseudonyms just to make my story more readable.

I want the reader to get a since of how God works in people's lives and uses hardships and setbacks to achieve a greater good.

So won't you join me and take a ride on an emotional rollercoaster called "Dale's life."

Index

~1~

Chapter 1

My mother had an extra marital affair and gave birth to my older half brother. My dad was furious at the situation, but nevertheless tried to make the marriage work. That's when I came along. I was born in a small town in the heart of California in the year 1959.

I don't think my mother had the capacity to make me feel loved.

> *One can't give something away that they*
> *don't have.*

My parents divorced when I was around seven. I experienced forms of emotional, physical and sexual abuse from both parents. I started smoking at the ripe old age of seven. We moved from our small town in California to Los Angeles when I was eight.

Unloved and alone

From as early as I can remember, I felt unloved from my mother. She would come home from work, look at me from the doorway of the room, then walk away. I can remember standing in my crib, excited to see my mom, then crying as she walked away.

I grew up as one of society's latch-key kids. My parents basically gave me keys to the house so I could come and go as I pleased.

A violent divorce

Sitting with my mother at the bed, my dad came in and threw a knife in-between us and sticking in the headboard just inches from our heads.

My mother came home one day crying and screaming at my dad holding a forty-five revolver in her hand. They were shaking terribly as she points it at him, threatening to shoot him. I was around seven years old at the time. I hid under a table with my friend, not really grasping the gravity of the situation. I don't know if my friend was real or imagined, but we pretended like we were shooting guns at the bad guy.

My dad always had crutches with him as he was an amputee. One day threatening to hit my mother with them, she grabbed me and used me as a shield in an attempt to save herself.

Sex abuse

My mother would have sex with her man friend in a studio apartment while I was in their trying to sleep. She would drag me from one place to another making me feel like a piece of luggage. Like she would be better off not having to take care of me.

During their divorce my parents would have sexual relations in the front seat of the car while I was in the back seat. My dad would tell me to get down on the floor. I thought I had done something wrong and I was being punished.

Smoking

I started smoking cigarettes when a friend brought several cartons with him to our hiding spot. His parents apparently were sales representatives for big tobacco companies and had scores of cigarette cartons just lying around. We smoked different brands and noted how dizzy we were after each one. Now being hooked on nicotine, I would walk to the store after school and steal a pack of cigarettes.

Funny thing is that store is still there and I frequent it often, as it's only a block away from where I live.

My dad's death

My dad passed away from cancer when I was ten years old. I cried when I heard the news and my brothers forbade me to cry because he was very abusive towards them.

> *I on the other hand, being the youngest,*
> *felt like I had lost my only friend and the*

only person in the world who loved me
unconditionally.

The unloved, being afraid and alone feelings would be with
me for the rest of my life. I learned to use drugs and alcohol
to numb the emotional pain I felt inside.

~2~

Chapter 2

I learned that I could cope with the pain through the use of drugs and alcohol. I grew up in the sex-drugs and rock-'n'-roll culture of the sixties. We always had plenty of concerts and parties to go to. I felt young and attractive to the opposite sex, until, that is, I met Nikki.

The neighborhood I grew up in was in the suburbs of Los Angeles where they had plenty of gangs and gang activity. I can't say I had a choice when it came to joining the gang or not. I could either suffer ridicule and humiliation from them everyday or I could join them.

Drugs

Drugs were a part of my everyday life from the age of seven to fifteen. It's amazing that I had a brain left after so much abuse.

Marijuana

I was introduced to smoking marijuana when I was around seven years old. My older brother shared a joint with me while I was hanging out with him and is girlfriend.

LSD

I took my first hit of LSD when I was around twelve. It was at a schools out for summer party.

Barbiturates

Reds or downers we called them.

Cannabinol

Cannabinol is an extract from the THC found in marijuana. It is the chemical that numbs your body and gets you high. We would snort it like cocaine. I had to have been around 14 years old when I first tried it.

I was so high one day that I fell down in the living room because I couldn't move any muscles. I could hear and see everything happening around me but I just lay there on the floor. My mom came home and asked what was wrong with me. My brother told her that I had snorted too much cannabinol.

> She asked, "will he be ok?" He said "yes".
> She said "Oh ok" and proceeded to step
> over me and walk away.

Concerts

Led Zeppelin, Humble Pie, James Gang, Robin Trower and Kiss. They were all held at the Long Beach Arena. We would get tickets in advance and show up ready to party. I would have my share of grass, hash and a boot legged bottle of whiskey. Yes, I would literally carry a bottle of whiskey in my boots.

Parties

A couple of fifteen and a half year olds were running away from home and stayed at our house for a few days. They were two twin girls with big breasts and busy long hair. Their first night there, my brother and some friends, went on a beer run and left me home alone with the girls.

> *By the time they got back, I had them*
> *dancing in the living room in just their*
> *underwear.*

The next night I was flirting with them and they suggested we have a threesome. As we were engaging in sex, a girl whom I was trying to get with, became very jealous. But for some reason I never hooked up with her.

Nikki

She was thirty two years old and I was twelve. My twelfth birthday was coming up and she wanted to throw this big party for me. I had some friends over and we did the normal birthday things; you know cake, presents and drinking. She kept telling me she had a special birthday gift for me, but she would only give it to me at the end of the night.

That's when she told me to undress and get in bed and lay on my back.

*She told me she was going to have sex
with me and that was her surprise
birthday present.*

I made arrangements with my mother's permission to move
in with her. My mother was unaware of the fact that we
were having sex. She thought that it would be good for me to
be with someone who could pay more attention to me than
she could.

Nikki and I would talk about the life we wanted to have
together. Her buying a ranch house and motorcycles for me
to ride all around the property all day. We continued to have
sex on a nightly basis.

As much as a twelve year old could love someone, I fell in
love with her. Then I discovered somethings about her I
didn't like. She liked to drink Scotch and would routinely pass
out after a few drinks.

Sometimes after work, she would bring John's home with her
to have sex for money. She worked as a waitress in a
restaurant and she had a way about her that attracted men.
Our relationship however continued on for a few weeks.

She would tell me stories about how her son was taken away
from her because they accused her of sexual abuse.
Apparently he was younger than I was and she was facing
sexual abuse charges.

As time went on she met one of my best friends who was
sixteen at the time. They immediately hit it off and off to the

bedroom they went, leaving me to sleep on the couch instead of in bed with her.

The next day police raided the house and arrested my friend for being a runaway and her for harboring a runaway.

The police officer looked at me and asked, "what are you doing here?". I said "I live here." He asked, "do you go to school?". I said, "yes". He said, "well go to school".

I can't express to you the level of hurt I felt that night. What she did was wrong.

I realized that at my age I didn't have the coping skills needed to adequately deal emotional loss.

As I mentioned beforehand, one of the ways I would deal with loss was to attempt to see my loved one again. At thirteen years old with my bicycle in route, I would ring her phone from the payphone outside her apartments. Crying on one end getting nothing but rejection from the other. I was very distraught. If that wasn't enough pain, on my way home, still crying from my loss. Then BAM! I hit a board or log or something. The street lights were out and it was very dark outside. I went "End-over-end" hitting the street doing, what I call "the asphalt ballet."

Sharing this part of my story I would get mixed messages. "You should be grateful for having sex with an older woman when you were young".

Often times I wondered; would the
response be different, if I was a young girl
and she was an older man?

Sadly to say, I think it would be different. Maybe in your generation it wouldn't matter, but in mine it did.

Gangs

The activities of the gang I was in included harboring runaways, girls pulling trains, partying, drinking, getting high and doing drugs. We would drive around in our low riders, looking for chic's or any trouble we might find. If we thought we might encounter other rival gangs, we would have guns at the ready. I personally carried a single shot 20 gage shotgun with a breakaway barrel. By God's grace I never had to use it, but there were a few times, I came very close.

I told someone one time about being in a gang as part of my past. He asked, "What did you guys do? Play tetherball?"; attempting to minimize my experience.

NLZ

The Nazi Low Riders was a gang I grew up with in Los Angeles. I received an initiation tattoo on my arm when I was thirteen. The sign of Nazi Germany's SS. We wore clothes similar to many Mexican gangs at the time. Dopey sandals, Pendleton shirts and kakis pants. Opening in the shirt so you could see the T-shirt underneath from the bottom up, with the top button buttoned. Hair cut short and combed straight back.

Rape's

There was one member in our gang that was in and out of juvenile hall on rape charges. He raped a girl one time at one of our parties. While we didn't condone it we also didn't stop it. He attempted to raped one of my girlfriends one knight with a knife right in front of me. He tried to stab her a few times but failed and he eventually gave up. He attempted to rape Nikki one time. She cried for me to help her, while I exclaimed "What do you want me to do?". He was 15 and I was 13, much bigger and more of a badass than I was. Fortunately, she put up a fight and he eventually gave up.

Rape is never about sex. It's about power and control.

> The one who has the most power in any
> relationship is the one who loves the least.

Train's

No not that kind of train, the kind of train that a girl pulls with several guys in line. We had our share of trains with girls mostly looking for a place to hide after they had run away from home.

One in particular stands out. We let her shack up in our garage for a few nights. One night she offered to perform oral sex on several of us guys just hanging out. It was completely dark and you couldn't see a thing. One guy would step up, she would do her thing, he would finish and the next guy would step up.

> When it was my turn, I stepped up and
> pulled it out. She says to me in a sexy
> voice, "oh hi Dale".

Jewelry heist

In an effort to rob a Woolworth's store, I set off a bomb as a diversion, while other members of the gang would attempt to steal jewelry. The bomb was homemade of course, made by fifteen year olds. It had smoke bombs, fountain fireworks and Piccolo Pete's all attached to a single fuse.

We decided on the location of the bomb placement, the further most point from where the jewelry cases were. My job was to simply light the bomb and make my escaped from the store. I lit the bomb and immediately ran out the back doors. I had no idea what happened after that.

Long story short, my homeboys were quickly apprehended by the store's security staff.

> *My bomb caught some merchandise on*
> *fire and killed a bird and a hamster.*

No charges were filed against me because I was only 13 at the time and only following orders from my older accomplices.

Although the drug use, going to concerts and parties were fun and exciting they were also beginning to take a toll on my life. But at least God somehow saw fit for me to get away from the gang. I went to foster care and afterwards moved away.

~3~

Chapter 3

My mother was beside herself when it came to raising me. I was always getting into trouble. She would say to me

"Dale, what am I going to do with you!"

She tried cutting my hair, foster care and eventually moving away. And after all of that, I still managed to have one last rendezvous with Nikki.

I believe God uses our hardships and setbacks to achieve a greater good and his is exactly what happened to me while exploring the Malibu Canyons with two girlfriends.

Foster care

I ditched school one time for two weeks straight, my mother realizing she could no longer take care of me and sent me away to live with a foster care family. I was upset at first, that once again my mother was abandoning me, but after awhile I felt secure and safe in the family structure they had to offer. I stayed away from old friends and refrained from smoking, drug use and alcohol.

This particular time in my life gave me a since of security through a family structure. I would come home for lunch, go back to school. No detours or I would get in trouble. Come home from school, do my homework, then eat dinner. Afterwards was some family time watching TV or just hanging out. Then bedtime, get up the next morning and do it all over again.

I would eventually leave the foster home and rejoin my family after they moved away from the gang neighborhood I was involved with.

I think I missed structure in my life
growing up and for a short time, I had it.

It was a safe and comfortable feeling without fear or trauma. Something I told my mom I would get by moving in with Nikki, but of course, that never happened.

New Scenery

We moved away from the neighborhood to a coastal one, and away from the gangs and people I would hang with. I'd like to say that I stayed out of trouble and away from hoodlums, but I didn't.

One day a classmate, for some reason didn't like me and chose to pick a fight with me. He unlatched his belt and proceeded to attempt to hit me with it. Coming from where I came from, fighting was no stranger to me. I grabbed the belt from him, thru him to the ground and kicked him with my hiking boots.

Later that day, it turns out this kid was associated with a gang in that school. The head of the gang approach me in the hallway and pinned me up against a corner with six other gang members standing behind him. He told me that he was going to kick my ass for what I had done to his homeboy. I told him it was his homeboy who started the fight, and I was just defending myself. My reasoning fell on deaf ears as he pushed me once again against the wall. So I told him,

> *"You're all big and bad when it's one*
> *against seven, let me get my friends*
> *together so we can have a fair fight."*

It was agreed, we would meet after school to settle this.

Now, I'm sure by this time, you all can only imagine who my friends were. They were two brothers. Both of them never wore a t-shirt or shoes. Their hair was bushy and hung down past the middle of their backs, they only stood about five eight, but you could tell these guys meant business. They happened to be well trained kung fu fighters, and were not afraid to use it in the streets. The day we were supposed to fight, my friends and I showed up and nobody from the gang wanted to fight us. From that day on, I never had anymore problems with them.

Rendezvous

I was now fifteen and a half and had my driver's permit. Some of my old gang member friends came to party at my house after we had moved from the neighborhood. My friend that Nikki hooked up with was there and offered to give me her phone number. I ended up seeing her one last time.

I drove myself to her apartment. She greeted me and introduced me to a fifteen and a half year old runaway she had staying there. The more things change, the more they stay the same. She retired to her bedroom with her John. I ended up having sex with the runaway, not Nikki.

> We had sex all night long and I came in
> her five times, without pulling out. As far
> as my sex life goes, it was all down hill
> from there.

They say that men reach their sexual peak at eighteen while women reach their peak at the ripe age of thirty-two. I have had sex with more women/girls by the time I was sixteen that most guys have had all their lives.

Malibu canyon

I've always had a thing for blonds. I "borrowed" my mother's car and took a couple of blond girlfriends for a joy ride. It was a baby blue Volkswagen VW. I had a crush on one of the girls and thought it would be an opportunity to impress her if I took her to Malibu canyon. We parked the car and went for a walk down a dried up riverbed. We stopped and smoked a couple of joints I had prepared before the trip. She didn't pay the kind of attention to me that I had wanted, so I immediately copped an attitude and demanded we go home. I took off like a bat-out-of-hell and lost control of the car.

We veered off the dirt road and drove
over the side of a cliff.

Before going all the way down we hit a tree and hung there in the balance. The first thing I did was freak-out. I was fifteen years old and didn't have a driver's license. My mother was going to kill me, I thought. I got out of the car and fell several feet through the tree and brush. After coming to a stop I climbed up the side by grabbing tree limbs and bushes to aid my ascent. The girls freaked out as well and managed to get out of the car and position themselves on the hood screaming and yelling. Not being able to calm myself down, I ran hysterically across the canyon. After awhile, a thought came over me:

"everything is going to be ok".

About that time, I saw headlights on a car in the distance. It was the girls. They found help at a house nearby and went out searching for me. The good neighbors were able to give us a ride home.

My mother was more "matter of fact" about retrieving the car than wanting to punish me. So with the aid of a towing company we got the car out of it's predicament and towed it home. Damage to the car was more superficial than structural, so we got the repairs done and that was that.

Some kind of a spiritual awakening
occurred in me that day.

The experience ended up having a profound impact and literally changed my life. I stopped using drugs, smoking cigarettes and marijuana and I stopped drinking. I started going to church, participating in sports and doing well in school. I went from D's and F's to A's and B's on my report cards.

~4~

Chapter 4

High school was a time for me to find my identity, explore different subjects and sporting activities and find out what I liked best in life. I came along way from being a hoodlum to becoming an All American student. I attribute this to staying away from gangs, going to church and doing well in school.

Just after junior high school I went on a thirty day tour of Europe and visited five different countries. I became school President, went to boys state and received two scholarships to college.

Europe

I had the opportunity of a lifetime to join the Foreign Study League on a thirty day trip to Europe, but the cost was too high. One of the faculty members leading the group heard about me and my desire to join them and offered to pay my way. I'll never forget the day I found out about this and how excited I was to be going to Europe.

London

After flying from Los Angeles to New York City, we made our way across the pond over night and landed in London. Our first stop was the Tower of London. We took a tour and learned that back in 14th and 15th century they had a way of dealing with suspected witches. They would tie stones to their bodies and throw them in the river. If they drowned, they weren't witches, but it they floated, they were. Then they would kill them for being a witch.

The changing of the guards was quite the spectacle to see with all of it's pageantry. The queens guards are the men with the big furry hats and red uniforms. Each guard is a minimum of six foot seven inches tall and with their hats they look over seven feet tall.

We met with one of the guards after he got off work and had lunch with him. With his English accent he would make references to the "bloody this" and the "bloody that. He would use the word "bloody" in the way us Americans use the word "fuck" and "fucking".

One day we took a trip to see Windsor Castle. It's amazing the rich history England has and the buildings are a testament to that.

The Eiffel Tower was spectacular and the Arc de Triumph are Paris landmarks that are must sees. I walked for it seems like forever to get a look at the Mona Lisa.

Rome

We stayed in a convent in Rome, right next door to a prison. A garden was positioned on a hill with a breath taking view of

Rome. But in contrast you could see the prison with guards holding machine guns on the roof.

It was amazing to me that you could walk through Rome and just stumble across ancient ruins.

The Sistine Chapel is a church located in Vatican City. I can't even begin to tell you how beautiful Michelangelo's paintings are on the ceiling.

Michael Angelo's Mary and Christ statue, Pieta, had been vandalize a few years prior to our visit. You could see how they had put some of the broken pieces together. The foot of the virgin Mary was missing toes, not because of damage, but because visitors would touch her foot and pray. After millions of parishioners her foot was missing toes.

Pompeii was amazing because you could see castings of people that had died during Mount Vesuvius's eruption. Stone block roads still had chariot wheel impressions in them. Several blocks of roads and houses have been preserved by the eruptions ashes.

Gondolas in Venice are so iconic that I bought a gold necklace with a Gondola on it as a gift for my Mother.

The Statue of David in Florence is bigger that anyone can imagine when you see it in person. Just the base alone is taller than people standing next to it.

Munich

I saw a Church in Munich that has a clock that is a carousel of life size dolls that chimes every hour. Another memorable moment in Munich is I ran up the steps of the Olympic ski jump.

Madrid

I discovered one of my favorite dishes in Spain. The paella is a dinner dish made up of rice, chicken, lobster, snails and oysters. I'm not big on oysters but I love snails, delicious.

I went to a zoo outside the city of Toledo location of the museum of El Greco. It's interesting to note that there are several roman ruins located there as well.

I can't express how valuable this whole experience was. My studies in college were filled with references to Europe. In my history and art classes I had a direct connection to the things we studied because of this experience. It made my studies more meaningful because I could say "I've been there" and "I saw that".

School President

I had a friend in school who wanted to run for vice-president of the school and asked me if I would run for president. I agreed and we began our campaign as a two man team on one ticket. I made speeches in front of the school and created gimmicks to help our campaign. I was running up against a girl who had a solid following and experience in student body leadership.

The day came for the election and the votes were tallied. It was so close that the committee called it a tie. We were given another week of campaigning followed by a run off vote. This time I was the winner without question.

I will never forget the learning opportunities I had through that experience and am very grateful for everything it taught me.

Boy's State

Each year one student from each school is nominated to attend Boys State, held at Sacramento State University in California. I was awarded the nomination. It's a place where students run for office and hold meetings similar to how the state government is ran. We also competed in sporting events like football, track and field, basketball and baseball.

It was a great honor to attend there and I learned a great deal about how our government is run through the process. I also learned that politics was not something I wanted to pursue because I didn't have the magnetism needed to gain peoples votes. And at this point I didn't know what I wanted to do in life, nor what I wanted to focus on in my studies.

Scholarships

Every year a scholarship was awarded to a student with outstanding achievements in sports, academics and leadership. I'm proud to say that I was granted that scholarship. In addition to that, I was also granted a scholarship from the college I wanted to attend in Illinois.

I applied to several military academy's, West Point, Annapolis and the Air Force academy. I got as far as receiving a congressional nomination to West Point. This was quite the accomplishment since the only a handful of nominations are given out.

I'm very proud of my achievements, given what I had been through growing up. God only knows where I was headed had I not changed the path I was on. Life was good and it was about to get better in the next few years.

~5~

Chapter 5

In college I spent time finding myself and my identity. I was in love with my high school sweetheart. I had an exciting future as a college athlete. I danced my way through college and dated several women along the way. I had an internship in Washington DC with the United States Chamber of Commerce. And to top it all off, I went to Colorado Springs to get special training in the field of computer science.

Finding my niche

My first day of college went like this, during a freshmen mixer I walked up to a group of people and asked them "who died!" they replied "well actually someone did die." Please place foot in mouth.

I had a short athletic career because of my knee injury. But this gave me time to focus on other things. I initially wanted to get my degree in engineering, but the college only offered a two year program. I had to make a decision, leave the college after two years, or change my major. Because of the scholarship program I was in, it made since for me to stay for four years and change my major. Computer Science Studies were limited to a two year program as well, so I opted for a Bachelor's of Arts degree in Business Administration.

My English professor once asked me "what is your major?", I said "Business Administration with a Computer Science Minor". He said

"good, stick with computers"

High school sweet heart

I met her in church when I was eighteen and she was sixteen. She was a ballet dancer and had a flair for the dramatic. We attempted to continue our relationship while in different states across the country. She went to New York University while I was in college in Illinois. Our love was short lived as she soon met someone in New York that she would end up falling in love with. When she gave me the news I was heartbroken.

Losing loved ones in my life was difficult and traumatic.

I never really dealt with my grief from my childhood, so it made it even more difficult for me to deal with it as an adult.

One of the things I would do is show up at lost love's doorstep in an attempt to rekindle the relationship.

I took the train from Illinois to New York and paid her a surprise visit. But all this did for me was make the hurt and pain worse. It would take me years to get over her.

Football

It was my freshman year in college and I was designated team captain. Having the fastest legs on the team and the best hands for receiving, most of the time the plays called involved me running or catching the ball. I also played strong side cornerback on defense. It was an honor and a privilege to play with the group of guys I played with. We didn't win many games but we all got to play. There were only about thirty guys on our team and we went up against schools with eighty guys on theirs.

Towards the end of the game, when we were clearly going to loose, the other team would send in players with clean jerseys. So we would make light of the situation and call ourselves

"the dirty thirty".

It was early in my sophomore year when I sustained an injury to my left knee. That marked the end of my athletic career as my performance was never the same.

Track and field

I ran the 400 meter and was a pole-vaulter. After my knee injury however I had to quit the team, because when I tried to run at my peak, my leg would cramp up, resulting in a pulled hamstring. Anyone who knows will tell you, that it is extremely painful.

Dances and dating

To relieve the stress of school work, we would regularly have dances. I loved women, so in order to get closer to them, I had to learn to dance. This was where I learned to swing dance. I would swing my way into the hearts of my chosen queens, so I thought. We held a special dance we called "the funk break". We played songs like Wild Cherry's "Play That Funky Music", George Clinton's "Atomic Dog", The Commodore's "Brick House" And Animal House's "Shout".

I actually only dated a couple of women from the college. I dated one other woman who was the daughter of one of my professors and another one who was visiting from Brazil. Of course one of the women was older and the others were younger. We had our normal romance and eventually the romance would fade.

The daughter of one of the professors was a school teacher some years older than me. If the professor found out about our romance, there would have been trouble for her to face. So we kept our relationship hidden from everyone, for the most part.

I met a girl from Brazil at a hospital I was working at when she visited her sister. Her sister was one of my coworkers. That romance only lasted until it was time for her to return to Brazil. I used to call her "Succolentte" which means "very juicy" in Brazilian.

I was at a friend's house one day and met a woman from out of town. We hit it off and ended up having sex in his backyard by the pool.

He had this dog that wanted to play fetch
while we having sex.

He would place the ball behind me, in-between my legs.
Frustrated with his ill-timed game of fetch, I would grab the
ball and throw it back in the pool. Sure enough, he would
dive in the pool, fetch the ball and bring it back again. We
laughed hysterically at the situation. The dog was not giving
up so we gave up and just hung out in the hot tub together.

Internship
For the first semester of my senior year I had an opportunity
to enter into an internship with the United States Chamber of
Commerce in Washington DC.

It was an exciting time in US politics. The year was 1982.
Ronald Reagan would be sworn in to his presidency and the
Iran hostages would return to the US.

I became an assistant speech writer for the chamber. Being
off campus, however, gave me a chance to get into trouble.
Friday and Saturday night I would frequent the bars in George
Town and go bar hopping. Well for me however, it was drink,
puke and lay my head somewhere so I could sober up,
instead of hopping from bar to bar.

Colorado Springs
Having completed the requirements for my business degree
early, I decided to concentrate my studies in Computer
Science. The college offered an extended program for

computer science off campus in Colorado Springs, CO. So for my last semester in college I went to Colorado.

The training I received there became the basis for my career as a computer programmer.

But unfortunately, while I was away from the college campus, I picked up smoking cigarettes and marijuana and drinking again. In addition, Colorado Springs was a military town and had the best strip clubs you could find anywhere in the country.

All-in-all, my college career was a success, minus a couple of set backs. I made the deans list in the last two years and despite my drinking and using again I did managed to graduate.

~6~

Chapter 6

It was the summer of 1982 and the country was in a recession. I graduated college, met a girl and got engaged. I finally found work in my field of choice, but still there was something missing.

I did ok as long as I was working, but as soon as I got off work I felt alone and worthless and began to drowned my feelings in alcohol. Because of my staying out late drinking I missed several days of work and was eventually fired from my programming job.

Graduating

The time after earning my degree and finding sobriety only lasted a couple of years. Although it was short, it did teach me that alcohol and drugs were not the solution.

I learned that any alcohol or drugs use
would trigger my alcoholism and drug
addiction all over again.

In order for me to be happy, joyous and free, I needed God and sobriety in my life.

After graduating college I looked for work in the computer software field, but no one was hiring because of the 1982 recession. I eventually would move in with my parents while I looked for work.

I got a job at a local junior college as the manager of the Computer Aided Training Department. Trust me, this was a brand new development in education as Apple Computers were barely two years old in the making.

After developing software that basically made the department run itself, the Dean of Vocation took notice and helped me get a job with a local software company.

That was the break I needed in order to
get my programming career off the
ground.

Engagement

I met a girl on her way to Hollywood. I will call her Susan. She was the sister of a girl I once new in college. I had seen her before at a school dance, but never actually met her.

Somehow she ended up in a small town near me. God or coincidence?

My mother met her in church and arranged a meeting. It was love at first sight. We dated for a while then decided to get married. I made arrangements to have our marriage ceremony in a glass church in Monterey. Our wedding celebration was going to be located in a reception hall at Pebble Beach.

Then I found out she was still in love with someone else. He was a Hollywood actor and new in the acting business. I found out about him because he called her one day and I answered the phone. This was back in the day when we only had land lines, no cell phones.

"Hello, is Susan there?" he asked, in a low resonating voice. After their conversation, of course, I asked her who he was. They used to date each other in college, but he moved on to become this famous actor. I asked her "do you still loved him and she said "yes". I asked her "would you go back to him if he asked you?". She said "yes".

I have always been an all or nothing kind of guy, when it came to love. It was one of those red flags in our relationship that I couldn't ignore.

Her father found out about our living together, and said he would not condone the marriage unless she had her own place. So she moved out and got her own place. That's when our relationship and our marriage plans began to go south. And of course it didn't help that my drinking was affecting my moods, decisions and behavior.

We got in a huge fight one day and I ended up slapping her. She didn't deserve that and I felt ashamed of how I behaved.

I would see her around town and my heart would sink every time I saw her. She eventually would end up moving away, but it took me years to get over her.

Alcoholism

After working for the company for only two years and because of my alcoholism, I got fired.

I got drunk one night and was kicked out of the bar. I went outside and kicked a wall down, took the bricks from the wall and smashed the bar owners car windows.

The next day my mom called me, told me to pay for the damages as she worked at the bar and didn't want to lose her job. She also told me to start going to meetings.

Fired

Not too many people can say they were fired from a job and almost "fired on" at the same time. I had been given several warnings at work, that if I didn't make it to work on time because of heavy drinking the night before, that I would be terminated.

The job I had was the first computer programming job I had after graduating college. I really liked it and I made good money with benefits. Being a full blown alcoholic and not knowing how to manage my drinking, I was destined to fail.

It was a Sunday night following the Super Bowl Sunday football game. My friends and I of course thought that it would be fun to hang out at the bar after drinking all day during the game. Having completely and utterly blacked out, the only thing I remember was who won the game. It was the Bears over the Patriots.

I woke up Monday morning, around 10:30 am, lying on the hallway floor. Oh my God, I thought, I think I blew it. I missed work once again. Where were my keys, where was my wallet? Wow, how could I have gotten so wasted. I went outside to see if my car was in the parking stall, it was. I looked for any signs of damage, blood stains on the fenders, that sort of thing. Nope, no damage, no hit and runs.

Later that day my friends showed up and explained to me what happened, where my things were and how I ended up crashed out on the floor. I knew at this point it was fruitless to call into work and tell them I wouldn't be coming in. So I just showed up the next day as if nothing happened.

A few minutes after I sat down at my desk, the boss called me in to his office.

There he was with a rifle in his lap. He said, "you're fired.", as he began to write out my last check. He told me,

> *"if you try anything, this gun may not kill*
> *you, but it'll sure slow you down".*

That's when I knew I had a drinking problem I that I needed to do something about it. I was at step one in my recovery.

> *"Admitted we were powerless over alcohol*
> *-- that our lives had become*
> *unmanageable".*

I earned my college degree, got engaged and found employment. Next thing I know I'm single, unemployed and at the end of my rope with my drinking. Fortunately for me, however, now I had a course to follow that would get my life back on track. I would find recovery, employment and romance in the years to come.

~7~

Chapter 7

I started going to meetings on a regular basis and began listening to the advice of the people with sobriety. Being sober allowed me to become employable again. I not only managed to sustain my career but got married as well.

Sobriety

One of the greatest accomplishments in my life was being able to maintain my sobriety for over thirteen years. With the help of God, going to meetings and activities with other sober members, I managed to stay clean and sober.

It wasn't until I became completely honest with myself that I found sobriety. I had applied for a job and when asked how I had lost my last job, I without hesitation said "work was slow and they laid me off". Of course this couldn't be further from the truth.

After some soul searching, I contacted the potential employer again and told them the truth about my alcoholism and how I was now in recovery. Admiring my honesty they hired me on as one of their programmer analyst.

Employment

I continued to work for that company for over nine years. After that I worked for a company based in Santa Monica, CA. From there I would work for a Fertilizer company as their IT Manager and then on to a Dairy Software company. The circumstances surrounding my job transitioning was uncanny.

The main programmer that provided software for the fertilizer company suddenly had a heart attack and died, leaving them in a bad situation.

They heard about me when I contacted them regarding possible upgrades to their system. They immediately hired me to not only maintain their system but to rewrite a new year 2000 compliant system. I knew all to well the issues with non y2k compliant software because I had addressed these issues in previous work experience.

I did some moonlighting work for a company that provided the software for a Dairy Software company. The dairy company was looking to upgrade their existing system and my name came up as someone who could help them do that. Everything seemed to fall right into place when I needed work.

It was as if someone was orchestrating
events in my life and put me where I was
needed most.

1st Marriage

I met her at a party one night. We were having a sobriety celebration and we heard there was a party going on next door. A couple of us guys decided to crash it. I read about ways to pickup women so I decided to put one of them to the test.

When you see a woman you're interested in, smile at her from across the room, then look away. Do this a few times, then walk up to her and introduce yourself. That's it, I tried it and it worked. I got her phone number and we started dating.

After a few months we decided to get married. We both owned homes at the time, instead of selling one of the homes I decided to rent mine out and move into hers. A few months past and I started going to counseling. I was around thirty-two years old when we got married and this was the first time I ever saw a therapist.

The further I delved into my past, the more I realized how much therapy I needed. My wife was supportive of me in the beginning but as time went on and the more of my past I dug up the less supportive she became.

One day I found out that she had read my forth step.

*"Made a searching and fearless moral
inventory of ourselves."*

There were some things I had wrote down in my inventory that she just couldn't live with. Mostly involving the time I was with a gang between the ages of thirteen and fifteen.

We ended up getting a divorce just after one year of marriage.

Life wasn't perfect, but at least I was clean and sober and had a good job. As long as I stay sober I would find another romance along the way that would work out better for me in the long run.

~8~

Chapter 8

My second marriage proved to be more compatible with me than my first marriage. We did things together and enjoyed the same passions in life. We bought new car, went to strip clubs and sang karaoke together.

2nd Marriage

It was an absolute blessing to have my wife in my life. God knows I'm not an easy person to live with. I have my depressive moods and my ups and downs. It's a miracle it lasted for over ten years.

We got married after living together for about a year. I figured that if we could make it that long then it would be safe to get married. This was my second marriage while my first marriage only lasted a year. My wife tolerated my obsession with our 350Z, my addiction to strip clubs and dancers and joined me in my love for singing.

It was late in the year of 2003 when we got married. Instead of having a big wedding we eloped and got married at the

Elvis Wedding Chapel in Las Vegas Nevada. I hired a limousine to pick us up and drive us up and down the Las Vegas strip. We tipped the limo driver and walked the strip visiting several landmarks within the city. After announcing our marriage to my mom, she told us

"your wedding date is the same wedding anniversary date as mine and your dad's".

Wow, my mind was blown. God or coincidence?

Nissan 350Z

I purchased a Nissan 2003 350Z straight off the dealership show room floor. We drove the car from California to San Antonio Texas, to Oklahoma, then to Las Vegas Nevada and got married and then back to California. The car performed perfectly and we never had any issues with it. I never thought about doing anything with it until we attended an International Z Club Car Show in Los Angeles. Afterwards, modifying the car became an obsession of mine.

All guys love fast cars, I'm certainty no exception. I added twin turbos to the engine along with an enter cooler, boost control and gages for compression, heat and oil temperature. Performance wise, the stock car would pull a 240 horsepower to the crank shaft.

After installing the turbocharger it would pull about 400 horsepower to the wheels.

It needs to look good when it rolls down the road, so I had a custom paint job added with ghost flames and candy apple red paint. Then I added 21 inch chrome wheels to make the car really stand out. I also added a television screen and speakers with a sub woofer to the trunk of the car. I could play any laser disk and it would play on a small screen in the front and also on the larger screen in the rear. We were now ready to enter car shows and each cars show we entered we placed 1st, 2nd or 3rd.

I had the time of my life, taking it to car shows all across California. I wanted more enjoyment from the car so I bought another set of wheels for racing. I got some light weight 15 inch racing wheels with Hoosier racing slicks. I raced at Button Willow, AAA speedway, Sacramento raceway and Laguna Seca Raceway. Each time working on fine tuning the performance and posting faster times on the race track as well as in the quarter mile.

One afternoon after installing line locks on the car, I was at a red light in one of the busiest intersections in town. I engaged the locks, applying brakes to the front wheels and did a monster burnout, filling the entire intersection with smoke. I got pulled over by the cops and given a ticket for running a red light.

> *The only thing running a red light that night was the smoke from burning my tires.*

Strip clubs

When I first met my wife we became best friends and she would listen to my stories about my going to strip clubs. So after we got married, she would encourage me to continue to go, but now as a couple. Being the strip club connoisseur that I was, we went to clubs all across California. We would pay for lap dances for the both of us and watch each other enjoy the moment. What a trooper she was.

Karaoke

I met my wife in a Karaoke bar so we would continue going out, singing and dancing at the clubs. Sometimes we would sing duets that we practiced. We loved it so much we added a karaoke system at home.

Although I didn't stay clean and sober during our marriage, I did limit my drinking and only used marijuana for stress relief and relaxation.

I had a good ten years of marriage and my career had reached it's peak. Overall I couldn't have been happier in my life. But just as I felt on top of the world, once again, I would sabotage myself and revert back to alcohol and drug abuse. It didn't help either that my wife wanted to divorce me.

~9~

Chapter 9

I had underlying feelings of worthlessness and guilt that I never really healed from. And because of that I ended up getting divorced and became white single and free again. I coped with my feelings by using drugs and alcohol.

Divorce

My wife met someone at work and fell in love with him. She was working as a bartender at the time and had a triple-D breast enhancement to increase her liquor sales and tips. I wanted to get her a t-shirt that said,

"this is what $10K looks like."

One night she came home from work and served me divorce papers, outlining the split of our assets. I would keep the Harley and the Camaro, while she gets the dog and the bedroom furniture. Seemed fair except for having to pay her alimony.

Being set free to do whatever I wanted in the bar scene turned out to be disastrous for me. I would stay out until 5:00 am in the morning and come home, get a couple hours of sleep and go to work. One such morning, my now separated wife, climbs into bed with me, crying to for me take her back again.

She tells me that the guy she fell in love with died of a heart attack. This was just two weeks after our separation. God or coincidence?

My feeling however, was you made your bed, now lay in it.

Freedom

We eventually got our own separate apartments, so there I was free to do whatever I wanted. I managed to keep my job, amongst the drug use, drinking and staying out late.

I say being white single and free was a disaster for me, because I did nothing but get in trouble. My loss God's opportunity.

Three DUI's, driving on a suspended license, three motorcycle wrecks and being eighty-sixed from five bars. On top of all that, I had to pay fines for all of my misdemeanors.

The alimony became such a hardship that I couldn't afford to pay insurance and loan payments on my 2014 Camaro. If things couldn't get any worse, someone associated with a motorcycle club, out of spite, shot my radiator and engine block full of bullet holes.

The police took it apart and the dealership refused to fix it, because it was dismantled. So it sat in storage for months and racked up an enormous bill for storage fees. The loan company wrote the loan off as a loss, so the IRS added it to my taxable income for that year.

The financial hardships only got worse because the last day I worked was in June of 2017 when I ended up going to jail. Being a full blown alcoholic and drug addict made it nearly impossible for me to find another job. Not to mention I would have to explain to any potential employer how I lost my job and what I've been doing since then.

Addiction

The progression of my alcoholism and drug addiction went from a couple of grams a week, to a couple of eight balls. Despite loosing my apartment, car, motorcycle and everything I owned, I continued to make drinking and drug use a priority in my life. I even turned to drug sales to support my habit. After I left the crack house, started stealing drugs and became homeless.

Somehow through my divorce, going back to my drug and alcohol abuse, I still had more to learn. Apparently I had more to lose as well, because things were about to get worse. I needed a lesson in drinking and driving and I was about to earn my degree in that subject.

~10~

Chapter 10

As the saying goes, one isn't ready to get clean and sober until they hit rock bottom. After several DUIs, going to jail, losing my job and ending up in a crack house, homeless that I finally admitted I was powerless over my drinking and drug use.

Drinking and driving

Going to jail for DUI's and driving on a suspended license marked the end of my career as a professional computer programmer. I was ordered to sign up for community service for the second and third time. Struggling with maintaining my job, my alcoholism and drug addiction, made it extremely difficult for me to attend community service. So, as a result, I was issued a warrant for my arrest in two different counties.

DUI #1

I was hanging out at a bar with a girlfriend while she was working as a DJ. It was just before dawn when I drove across the street to put gas in my Camaro. The wind picked up something fierce and I got this feeling that something was going to end up bad.

She got off work and we decided to follow some people for an after hours party. We followed them but were going to lose them if we didn't run a red light. There wasn't anyone on the road at that time so there I went. Right behind me was a CHP officer who immediately turned on his lights and pulled me over.

He said he smelled alcohol so asked me where I came from and if I had been drinking. I of course gave him the old couple of beers story and he asked me to perform a sobriety test. Instead of writing me a ticket for running a red light he wrote me up for a DUI and took me to jail.

DUI #2

Just two weeks after my first DUI I was driving my girlfriend to another bars Halloween party. It was raining like crazy and as I was driving the light turned yellow. I thought if I try to stop I'll be halfway thru the intersection, so I ran the red light. Right at the same intersection was a cop who witnessed the whole thing and pulled me over.

My girlfriend was dressed as a black widow while I was dressed as the devil. The police asked if we had been drinking and of course I gave him the old couple of beers story. I asked the cop if I could just do the breathalyzer test and for go the sobriety test. Little did I know that after your first DUI in California you are considered over the limit of you have any alcohol in your system.

Instead of going to jail, my car was impounded and I was given another citation for DUI. Turns out the tow truck driver was heading in the direction of our next bar and gave us a ride.

DUI #3

I had been on the outs with my girlfriend and I saw her with another man at a motorcycle event at a bar. This put me in a bad mood and it put me on a mission to get drunk. Drinking and driving in a car is one thing, but drinking and driving while you're on a motorcycle is another. It's all bad!

A buddy of mine and I proceeded to go bar hopping that night on our Harleys. The last thing I know is I'm speeding away from the bar and was unable to negotiate the turn, so I hit the center median and crashed. I just clipped my foot peg on the curb and down I went, doing the "asphalt ballet ".

As I was attempting to get my bike off the ground, a Good Samaritan offered to help me. I got back on my bike and drove home. Turns out the "Good Samaritan " called 911 and followed me home. By that time the police found me in the garage and arrested me for DUI.

Driving on a suspended license

It was the day of a big bike rally in town, I packed up my gear and my girlfriend and I headed off down the highway. We passed a section that was under construction and of course there is always a CHP officer nearby. He saw that the tags on my bike had expired and pulled me over.

I hadn't been drinking but it was bad enough to be driving on a suspended license. The officer wrote me a ticket and could have impounded my bike, but decided to give me a break and allow me to drive it to the nearest highway off ramp.

Other close calls

For some reason I was running from the police on my Harley and stopped at a bar in an attempt to hide. It was after hours and the bar was closed. I knocked on the windows and asked the owner,

> *"help, help, the cops are chasing me! Hide me!"*

The owner opened the doors for me, but by that time the cops were there.

She pleaded with the cops not to arrest me. Because they never actually saw me driving they couldn't arrest me. They gave me a chance to arrange for a ride home, but I was so drunk that I couldn't work my phone. So instead of arresting me the just took me to jail until I sobered up.

I was out one night with a girlfriend at a bar. At the end of the night I gave her a ride home. I dropped her off and before I could get out of the neighborhood, a sheriff was in the middle of the street waiting for me and pulled me over.

They ordered me out of the car with my hands up. After a long ordeal they ended impounding my car and sending me on my way.

They could have arrested me for:

> 1-Driving on a suspended license
> 2-Driving under the influence

3-Open container
4-Drug paraphernalia
5-Expired and Stolen tags
6-No license and No insurance

But they didn't . I think that after realizing what was going on, they didn't want to do all the paperwork involved in arresting me or giving me a ticket. By God's grace.

1st County jail

One fateful night during a drug and alcohol bender, I slept in my son-in-law's car, parked in his driveway. My phone was dead so I couldn't call a taxicab. Not knowing it was me attempting to sober up, he called the police. Five cop cars and one police dog later, I ended up going to jail and was arrested for my warrants.

It was a Friday night when they put me in the holding cell. I spent the next two days in there and was finally processed on Monday and moved to the general cell blocks. There were mostly drunks that would be thrown in the cell.

There was only one water faucet and one commode. Filthy and disgusting hardly describes the condition the holding cell was in. There wasn't any place to lay down except the floor and a couple of benches. There were so many people in there sometimes it was standing room only. Some people would be released on their own OR or bailed out. My warrants were no bail warrants, so I wasn't going anywhere.

*One guy turned out to be cool because he
worked for a good riding buddy of mine.
God or coincidence?*

We talked about our communal friends and shared stories in relation to them. It past the time but still, I couldn't wait to get out of there and into the general population.

Are you a Wood? Are you a Wood? They kept asking me. I said "yes". They immediately started making my bed and putting my things together. The leader of the Woods was a big weight lifting guy. Cool as can be. We ended up being good friends. I was the only guy on the floor that could beat him in a game of chess, but he would beat me at least two out of three matches. Come to find out he also dated Hanna. My bed number was #72. Which meant I was the 72nd person in the chow line everyday. In other words I was last in line. I also found out that I had $72 on my books which was the amount of money I had on me when I was arrested. God or coincidence?

I tried calling my employer but to no avail. I would get the secretary and ask for her to accept my collect call, but she denied me. After a few attempts, she even told me to stop calling. I had a sinking feeling that was it. I had lost my job. I worked there for over six years. Why was I being treated this way? I had no idea how long I was going to be in for until I finally had a chance to see the judge.

Shackled from my ankles to my hands they walked us to the court room through a long tunnel from the jail to the court house. We were seated in a special section apart from the civilian population and were told not to talk to anyone on the other side. Seventeen days was the verdict, which meant I had to spend a another week in jail before being released. They would post notices for inmates being released and when the release date was. After they posted my notice I was stunned to find out I was being transferred to another county. This is where things get crazy.

2nd County jail

My cellmate, in the other county, was the son of my roommates boss. God or coincidence?

We had much in common and lots to talk about. We ended up being good friends both in and out of jail. My verdict for the charges of driving on a suspended license was 27 days. Half of that time and a three day early release meant I had to serve another two weeks. I read books, shared stories with my cellmate and played games of Battleship. The time actually went by fairly fast.

Crack house

Before becoming homeless I lived in a house with three roommates. We all used cocaine and had several friends over for some wild parties.

Women

Women would come and go. Some women would hook up with one of us and end up staying for the duration of the affair. Often times they would be escorted off the premises because their drug use had become debilitating. In other words, as we would say, they were "twacked-out". You could see the symptoms when they began to twitch and through their arms around for no apparent reason.

I had a rule, if a woman wanted free crack, they were asked to take their clothes off when getting high. Also, if a woman wanted to crash at my pad, she needed to be naked. No sleeping in my bed with your clothes on. If they were not ok with that, then there were other beds available for them to sleep in.

Selling cocaine

I became quite the popular guy when my coke sales increased. Selling a quarter ounce of coke in one night was not unusual. Dealing with nefarious individuals became the norm instead of the exception. We looked down on thieves, people looking for hand outs, and people looking for fronts. I had a rule, no fronts, no hand outs and you pay when you get the goods.

We also had a policy of no drug deals in the street. One has to come inside and stay for a while. We didn't want people coming in and out all the time. However, sometimes we were so busy that we ignored our policy, just to cut down on the number of people in the house. On a busy day or night we could have somewhere between ten and fifteen people hanging out and partying.

It's a miracle we never got busted by the cops and that was by God's grace. Even in light of going to jail and losing my job, I still hadn't hit my bottom yet. It was until I was homeless on the streets that I finally admitted to myself that I needed help. So I checked myself into a drug and alcohol treatment center.

I successfully completed the program and looked for employment but just didn't have knowledge and skills needed to compete with younger candidates.

~11~

Chapter 11

I decided to retire because finding work at my age was almost impossible. I continue to stay clean and sober. I live in a small town where I grew up and have hopes for a brighter future.

Retirement

I had hopes of maybe re-entering the job market, but I found it very difficult competing with younger candidates who have more state-of-the-art training than myself. I try to go to meetings and work the twelve steps, and accept the fact that I may never work again in my chosen profession.

I must remember that I put myself in that position because of the choices I made in the past.

Staying clean and sober

I found myself drug addicted and homeless and finally checked myself into a drug and alcohol treatment center. Ninety days seemed like an eternity at the time, but I made it because I had no other choice. It gave me the foundation needed for continued sobriety by getting me back into the twelve steps. There have been times I thought about using but the thought only brings me closer to God and strengthens my relationship with Him.

Where I'm at now

At present I'm a retiree living in a small town in California. I spent 36 years of my life as a computer programmer analyst. I have one roommate that I share a rent with. Things that happen in my life and people that I encounter go beyond coincidence and are evidence of how God works in my life. One of the many loves in my life was a girl I met who was 17 years younger than me. Hanna's story was a tragic one ending in her dying of an alcohol induced seizure in 2019.

Turns out one of her uncle's is now my roommate. God or coincidence?

I feel privileged and fortunate to have had the opportunity to get to know her and spend a short time with her. Suffering from childhood abuse resulting in alcoholism she never made it to recovery. Raped by her father at a young age left her with more than just scars of a physical nature. She attempted suicide once by hanging herself in a garage, only to be discovered by her cousin who cut her down and barely saved her life.

I struggle with depression myself. I have to at least attempt to get better or it will certainly kill me. The loss of family, jobs, homes and basically everything I ever owned leaves me with emotional scars that result in major depression. Losing my wife of ten years to a divorce marked the beginning of my life's downward spiral. Losing my job, going to jail, alcoholism and drug addiction were a direct result of not dealing with my emotional pain.

Being clean and sober is the foundation upon which I can build a happier more productive life.

At the same time I work very hard every day to keep my depression at bay and follow the advice of my doctors and therapists.

Final message

Abuse is wrong no matter how you slice it. Neglect and abandonment is a form of abuse. Statutory rape is wrong no matter what the age's are or what the sex is of the partners involved.

I escaped the emotional and physical pain through the use of alcohol and drugs. When I was clean and sober I immersed myself in my work to escape the mental anguish I felt inside.

If only I had help when I was younger in dealing with my feelings. Imagine how different life might have been, what decisions I would make and what people I would choose to be with.

If there is anything to be gained in writing this book, it would be the therapeutic value it has given me. Maintaining my sobriety, continuing to work with doctors and therapist are top priorities for me in my life.

I continue to live the eleventh step every day:

"...praying only for the knowledge of his will for us and the power to carry that out."

I pray this book will carry the message that no matter how bad your situation is, there is hope:

"Having had a spiritual awakening as a result of these steps, we tried to carry this message to others and practice these principles in all our affairs ".

God bless and God speed.

Made in the USA
Las Vegas, NV
22 June 2023

73775631R00036